WELCOME TO

WELCOME TO THE DOLLHOUSE

Todd Solondz

Faber and Faber
BOSTON · LONDON

A CIP record for this book is available from the Library of Congress.
ISBN 0-571-19050-2

All interior photos courtesy of Jennifer Carchman

Printed in the United States of America

The author is gratefully indebted to Stephen Pevner, without whose goodwill
and tenacity this screenplay would not have been published.

For my Mom and Dad,
who like books.

PRODUCTION NOTES

Although there is no sex, nudity, or violence in the movie, many parents were reluctant, if not unwilling, to allow their children to participate in it. Ann Goulder, the casting director, and I described the material as "unsettling," prompting some of the parents to retort, "sick" or "depressing," which I took as a compliment, as that reflected the world I was trying to portray. Unfortunately, there were many more parents who found the script "delightful," and this had me concerned, particularly when I could see the forced frozen smiles of their children.

Ann and I spent many weekends combing the malls in New Jersey, handing out audition flyers to eleven-year-old girls who showed signs of self-loathing and misery and thirteen-year-old boys who looked mean and like they could beat me up. For the most part, unfortunately, we found the kids were what they looked like. The role of Brandon McCarthy, consequently, had to be rethought, because the dumb and ugly types I was originally seeking turned out to be just too dumb and ugly.

Heather Matarazzo, the (then) eleven-year-old who plays Dawn Wiener, acted in almost every scene in the movie and had to be on set every day of the shoot. She is an extraordinarily vivacious and friendly girl, alternately "mature" and, naturally, juvenile. The fear was that Heather would lose interest in the movie after she discovered how tedious and dreary the film production process is and tell her mother midway that she'd rather enroll in basketball camp (her original summer plans). But, amazingly, she actually loved being on the set, and for as many hours as possible. Perhaps most remarkable of all, no one got sick of her.

The film was shot during the summer of 1994 in West Caldwell, New Jersey.

NOTE ON THE TEXT

The screenplay published here is a transcription of what finally appears in the movie. Many scenes were juggled around from, added to, or cut out of the original shooting script. A little—but very little—dialogue was improvised on the set. Perhaps I added a few extra "fucks" to Brandon's lines.

Many people have asked me about the "original" version of the script, and why and how I made changes. There were, in fact, several earlier drafts of *Welcome to the Dollhouse,* all darker and more depressing than the final version. It took time to find the right level of bleakness.

Once upon a time a friend performed a card trick for me. She repeated it many times, but I could never figure it out. I pleaded with her to reveal the secret to me, and she refused. She said it was magic. I became upset. When I relayed this to my psychiatrist he said he wouldn't want to know the secret: he liked to believe in magic.

I still don't believe in magic, but I like the idea of believing in it, and so I have chosen not to print any of the earlier drafts of my script.

Todd Solondz
June 1996

Welcome to the Dollhouse was first shown at the Toronto International Film Festival in September 1995.

Writer/Director/Producer	Todd Solondz
Executive Producer	Donna Bascom
Line Producer	Priscilla Guastavino
Co-Producers	Dan Partland
	Ted Skillman
Editor	Alan Oxman
Music	Jill Wisoff
Director of Photography	Randy Drummond
Production Design	Susan Block
Art Direction	Lori Solondz
Sound	Alex Wolfe
Casting	Ann Goulder

CAST
(in order of appearance)

DAWN WIENER	Heather Matarazzo
LOLITA	Victoria Davis
COOKIE	Christina Brucato
CYNTHIA	Christina Vidal
CHRISSY	Siri Howard
BRANDON MCCARTHY	Brendan Sexton, Jr.
JED	Telly Pontidis
LANCE	Herbie Duarte
TROY	Scott Coogan
MISSY WIENER	Daria Kalinina
MARK WIENER	Matthew Faber
KENNY	Josiah Trager
BARRY	Ken Leung
RALPHY	Dimitri Iervolino
MRS. GRISSOM	Rica Martens
MRS. WIENER	Angela Pietropinto
MR. WIENER	Bill Buell
STEVE RODGERS	Eric Mabius
MARY ELLEN MORIARTY	Stacye Moseley
MR. EDWARDS	Will Lyman
MRS. IANNONE	Elizabeth Martin
GINGER FRIEDMAN	Zsanné Pitta
MR. KASDAN	Richard Gould
STEVE'S GIRLFRIEND	Beverly Hecht
POLICE SERGEANT	Teddy Coluca
TOMMY MCCARTHY	Tommy Fager
MR. MCCARTHY	James O'Donoghue

TITLE SEQUENCE

A Chopin waltz begins.

A framed color photographic portrait of the Wiener family hangs on a wood-panelled wall. In it the smiling parents are surrounded by adorable MISSY, 8, *"awkward"* DAWN, 12, *and studious* MARK, 16. *The* CAMERA ZOOMS *into a close-up of* DAWN.

THE MUSIC ENDS AS THE PICTURE FADES TO BLACK.

INT. BENJAMIN FRANKLIN JUNIOR HIGH SCHOOL CAFETERIA—DAY

DAWN *stands in line with a tray, gets her food, and then looks about the room: where is she going to sit? She walks around, but wherever she spots an empty chair, she sees a table filled with unwelcoming kids.*

She finds one student (LOLITA) *sitting alone, and works up the courage to ask to sit down with her.* LOLITA, *detecting* DAWN*'s intent, is wary.*

> DAWN

Can I sit here?

> LOLITA
> *(A pause while she considers)* If you feel like it.

DAWN *settles herself opposite* LOLITA *and starts eating.*

> LOLITA

Someone barfed there fourth period.

DAWN *rises briefly, but then decides just to stay where she is and eat her meal in silence.* LOLITA *stares at her with menace.*

Suddenly a half-dozen pretty cheerleading girls approach, giggling. The prettiest one, COOKIE CUMMINGS, *manages to contain herself and put on an act of sincerity.*

> COOKIE

Hi, Dawn. Sorry to bother you, but we were just wondering. Are you a lesbian? *(No response)* Well, are you?

> DAWN

No.

4

LOLITA

Liar. (*To* COOKIE *and her friends*) She made a pass at me.

DAWN *is too stunned to say anything.* LOLITA *gets up and leaves the table.* COOKIE *and her friends follow, laughing and chanting, "Lesbo! Lesbo!" etc.*

INT. SCHOOL CORRIDOR—DAY

The CAMERA TILTS DOWN DAWN's *locker, which is smeared with mean "Wiener-dog" graffiti.*

It is pretty desolate. DAWN *is shutting her locker when suddenly she hears a tussle from around the corner.*

VOICE #1

. . . Aw, you little faggot . . .

VOICE #2

Look at Troy-boy!

VOICE #1

Fuckin' faggot, you're a faggot! Aren't you, Troy-boy? Aren't you?

VOICE #3

No!

VOICE #1

Say it: "I'm a faggot!"

VOICE #3

No!

She moves to investigate and discovers BRANDON MCCARTHY, 13-year-old class bully, and his brutish cohorts, JED and LANCE, beating up on TROY, class brain and weakling. She is horrified, but too scared to do anything except cautiously observe.

BRANDON

"I'm a faggot!"

TROY

No!

5

BRANDON

Admit it! Say it! "I'm a faggot!"

TROY

No!

JED

Say it, faggot!

TROY

No!

LANCE

Say it!

BRANDON

SAY IT!

BRANDON *twists* TROY*'s arm back an extra notch. The pain is now too unbearable.*

TROY

(*Barely audible*) I'm a faggot.

BRANDON

He said it! He said it! He admitted he's a faggot!

JED

I can't believe it! He really is a faggot!

DAWN

Why don't you just leave him alone?

JED

Hey, guys, watch out! It's the Wiener-dog!

BRANDON

Eww! It's Dogface!

DAWN

You guys are such jerks.

BRANDON

What's the matter, ugly? You like faggots?

BRANDON *gives* TROY *a final punch.* DAWN *watches helplessly.*

6

(*To* JED *and* LANCE) C'mon. Let's get outta here. Her face is killing me.

BRANDON, JED, *and* LANCE *leave, laughing.*

DAWN *turns to* TROY, *sunken on the floor.*

DAWN

Are you all right, Troy?

TROY

Leave me alone, Wiener-dog.

DAWN *watches as, bent over, he stumbles away.*

EXT. WIENER HOME—DAY

MARK *is rehearsing in the open garage with his all-guy rock 'n' roll band. But clearly they are an untalented lot. And clearly they are not "cool."* MARK *plays guitar,* KENNY *drums, and* BARRY *keyboard.* KENNY*'s drum set is inscribed with the group's name, "The Quadratics."*

MISSY, *wearing her ballet outfit (pink leotard, pink tutu), dances to their "music" on the driveway.*

KENNY

Hey, that didn't sound too much like "Satisfaction."

MARK

Yeah, what's the matter, do you think?

BARRY

I dunno. It says B-flat, I'm just playing what it says.

MARK

Play me an A.

BARRY *plays an A.* MARK *plays his out-of-tune A.*

KENNY

This is bad.

MARK

Yeah, we sound like shit.

7

> BARRY

I knew this band idea was gonna suck.

> MISSY

What does "suck" mean?

> MARK

Missy, go play with Dawn.

MISSY *leaves.*

> MARK

Now we've just gotta practice more. Hell, it's our first time. What do you think the Stones sounded like the first time they practiced?

> KENNY

Yeah . . .

> BARRY

Okay . . .

> MARK

Okay. Now I'm gonna close the garage door so we can get some privacy.

The garage door closes as we hear:

> MARK

Okay, let's take it from the top. One, and a two, and a one, two, three, four . . .

They resume their playing, but of course it still sounds terrible.

INT. TV ROOM—THAT MOMENT

DAWN *is drinking soda while watching a kids' quiz show on TV.*

> TV MC

Toss-up question: spell the word "Satellite."

> TV KID

S-a-t-e-l-l-i-t-e.

TV MC

That's correct. You got twenty points on that bonus.

MISSY *prances inside and stops by* DAWN.

MISSY

You know you're not supposed to drink in the TV room.

DAWN

Drop dead, lesbo.

A beat, then MISSY *goes into the kitchen.*

MISSY (O.S.)

Mommy, Dawn called me lesbo.

MRS. WIENER (O.S.)

(*Who has been chatting on the phone*) Hold on, Rita. (*Calling*) Oh,
Dawn! (*No response.*) Dawn, I want to speak to you right now!

DAWN *rises, muttering under her breath, and then leaves the room without turning off the TV.*

MRS. WIENER (O.S.)

What did you call your sister?

DAWN (O.S.)

She was bothering me!

MRS. WIENER (O.S.)

I don't care what she was doing. Now are you going to apologize?

DAWN (O.S.)

No!

MRS. WIENER (O.S.)

Apologize or you're punished!

DAWN (O.S.)

(*Stomping her foot*) But Mom, she was bothering me!

MRS. WIENER (O.S.)

(*Losing her temper*) No! No! That's it! Go to your room!

DAWN (O.S.)

She's such a little . . .

MRS. WIENER (O.S.)
Go! That's it! I don't want to hear it! Go!

A door slams (o.s.) Finally, a moment of silence, save for what's on TV. Then: MISSY *re-enters and turns the channel to QVC, the home shopping channel, where they are selling dolls. The* TV VOICE *says: "...Yeah...I love her little profile. That's so cute. Let's go to the phones..."*

EXT. WIENER HOME—THAT AFTERNOON

DAWN's *friend* RALPHY *rings the doorbell.* MISSY *opens the door slightly without unchaining it.*

RALPHY
Hi, Missy. Is Dawn home?

MISSY
Yeah, but she can't play. She's punished.

MISSY *slams the door in his face.*

INT. DAWN'S BEDROOM—THAT MOMENT

All the furniture and furnishings are bright, cute, and cheery.

DAWN *sits on her bed and clenches herself, seething with anger.*

INT. BENJAMIN FRANKLIN JUNIOR HIGH SCHOOL—DAY

The CAMERA DOLLIES *along an empty hallway.*

INT. CLASSROOM—DAY

MRS. GRISSOM, *the grammar teacher, slowly paces up and down the aisles of seats as the class takes a test. She is on the look-out for any cheaters.*

BRANDON *tries sneaking a look at* DAWN's *answers. She silently mouths to him to stop it, but he ignores her. Finally she raises her hand.*

DAWN
Mrs. Grissom?

MRS. GRISSOM

Yes, Dawn?

DAWN

Brandon's trying to copy my answers.

BRANDON

You lie!

DAWN

You were too and you know it!

Pell-mell breaks out.

MRS. GRISSOM

Quiet! (*Instant silence.*) Dawn. Brandon. You can see me here at three. I'm giving you both detention.

INT. GIRLS' LAVATORY—DAY

DAWN *enters just as* LOLITA *comes out of a stall. On seeing* LOLITA, DAWN *is taken off guard:*

DAWN

Oh! Hi!

LOLITA *says nothing, just stands by the sink and stares at her.* DAWN *starts washing her hands.*

LOLITA

You didn't come in here to wash your hands.

DAWN

Y-yes, I did.

LOLITA

You came in here to take a shit.

DAWN

N-no. Really. I-I don't have to go. My hands were just dirty, that's all.

LOLITA

Liar. I can smell you from here.

11

DAWN *tries to get by, but* LOLITA *won't let her pass.*

DAWN

Please let me go.

LOLITA

First take a shit.

DAWN

But I'll be late for science!

LOLITA

Well, you're not leaving until you do.

DAWN

You know, Lolita, me and my neighbor are starting this new club. And if you want you can be vice president.

LOLITA

(*Advancing ominously*) Fuck you.

DAWN

A-and I really wasn't the one who was cheating . . . I'm innocent.

LOLITA

I know. You're always innocent. And Brandon's always guilty.

DAWN

But Brandon *was* chea—

LOLITA

You stay away from Brandon. He's mine. Got it?

DAWN

O-of course, but—

LOLITA

But shit. Now go on.

LOLITA *shoves* DAWN *into a stall.* DAWN *tries to close the door behind her, but* LOLITA *won't let her.*

LOLITA

Leave it. I want to make sure you shit. I want to see it with my own eyes.

                              DAWN (O.S.)
Why do you hate me?

                                LOLITA
Because you're ugly.

EXT. SCHOOL EXIT—DAY

DAWN *comes tearing out and runs over to the school playing field, crashing to a halt at the wire fence. She pants.*

EXT. SCHOOL—DAY

Three o'clock: yellow buses and carpools fill up with the crowd of kids rushing out of the building.

INT. MRS. GRISSOM'S CLASSROOM—DAY

Detention: DAWN *and* BRANDON *sit on opposite sides of the room,* MRS. GRISSOM *at her big desk dead-center. She grades papers while the two detainees complete retests.*

BRANDON *silently mouths "fuck you" over and over at* DAWN. *He gives her the evil eye. He sends her lewd kisses.* DAWN *tries to hold her pencil straight, but she can't keep her hand from shaking. Finally, she raises her hand.*

                                DAWN
Mrs. Grissom? I'm finished.

                            MRS. GRISSOM
Let me see.

DAWN *walks up to* MRS. GRISSOM *and hands her the test.* MRS. GRISSOM *takes out her red pencil and briskly corrects it.* DAWN'*s grade:* D–.

                                DAWN
Mrs. Grissom, can I take a retest?

                            MRS. GRISSOM
No.

                                 13

DAWN

But I *know* I could've done better if none of this had happened. I was nervous.

MRS. GRISSOM

I said no, Dawn.

DAWN

But Mrs. Grissom, I really wasn't the one who was cheating and . . . if I could just redo this test . . . just once. . . . Please . . . I'm better than a D– . . .

MRS. GRISSOM

Stop grade-grubbing! Don't you have any dignity?

A beat. DAWN *is speechless.*

MRS. GRISSOM

Now I want you to write a hundred-word essay on the subject of dignity and hand it in to me by Friday. You're excused.

EXT. WIENER BACKYARD—DAY

The CAMERA PANS *from* MISSY—*prancing about on the lawn in her tutu—to* DAWN *looking out from her clubhouse. A sign reads* "The Special People Club."

RALPHY *is playing with some toy cars next to* DAWN.

DAWN
(*Watching* MISSY) She's got it so easy. She'll always have it easy.

RALPHY

Maybe she'll die.

DAWN
(*Sighing*) You don't know what it's like.

RALPHY

What?

DAWN

Junior high . . .

Pause.

14

Missy and Mrs. Wiener at dinner

> RALPHY
> Do you think anyone'll join our club?

> DAWN
> I don't want anyone to join. (*Pause*) I wanna be popular.

INT. KITCHEN—EVENING

Suppertime. The family sits around the table. DAWN *silently mouths "fuck you" over and over again, a la Brandon, at* MISSY.

> MARK
> So I think I may have swung a pretty good deal with Steve Rodgers today. I think we got him.

> MR. WIENER
> Who's Steve Rodgers?

> MARK
> Well, Steve Rodgers is only, like, one of the most popular guys in class. We get him, we'll get invited to play everywhere: sweet sixteens, school dances, maybe even get a gig on the road!

15

MR. WIENER

What instrument does he play?

MARK

Guitar, a little. But mainly he sings. But that's not the point. The point is is it's just exactly what I needed for my college resume. With this kind of substantial extracurricular activity I'm gonna have it made. Maybe not the Big Three, but an Ivy at least.

MRS. WIENER

Well, we'll have to see about those SATs.

MISSY

Mommy, can I join Mark's band?

MRS. WIENER

Aww, sweetheart!

MISSY

I'm serious. And I think you should send Dawn to a reformatory. She's *always* bothering me!

MRS. WIENER

Aww, honey, you don't mean that. Dawn loves you. Remember, no matter what she does, she's your sister. . . . Dawn, tell Missy that you're sorry for bothering her and that you love her. (*No response.*) Dawn . . .

DAWN

I'm not sorry.

MRS. WIENER

Stop acting like a baby. You're her older sister. And Missy loves you.

DAWN

She does not.

MRS. WIENER

Of course, she does. (*To* MISSY) Tell her that you love her.

MISSY

I love you.

DAWN

You do not!

MISSY

I do too!

DAWN

You do not—!

MRS. WIENER

DAWN! You are not leaving this table until you tell your sister that you love her!

EXT. WIENER HOME—NIGHT

The kitchen light is on.

INT. WIENER KITCHEN—NIGHT

DAWN *is still sitting at the kitchen table.* MRS. WIENER, *in a nightgown, shuffles in.*

MRS. WIENER

Go to bed.

DAWN *rises and leaves.*

FADE TO BLACK.

INT. DAWN AND MISSY'S BEDROOM—DAY

Bright daylight streams through the window as DAWN *saws off the head of one of* MISSY's *dolls. Suddenly she is struck by the distant sound of a young man singing. She rises to find the source:*

VOICE

(*Singing*) I'm taking candy from my baby
Sweet candy from my baby
I know you're daddy's girl but it don't worry me
Won't you give me some sweet candy . . .

INT. HALLWAY—DAY

As if in a trance, DAWN *walks along slowly, quietly descends the stairs. She passes by her mother, who is talking on the phone.*

MRS. WIENER (O.S.)

. . . Oh, well, Dawn is very musical . . . Yeah . . . Yeah, no, I
know . . . No, she's going . . . Well, I told her, she'll have a fabu-
lous time . . . I know, what kid doesn't want to go to Disney
World? . . . Right . . . right, yes, well . . . Um-hmm . . .

VOICE (O.S.)

(*Getting louder*) . . . Let's get a little wild
Let's get a little crazy . . .

EXT. WIENER HOME—DAY

DAWN *opens the front door and finally sees the owner of the voice: singer/
guitarist* STEVE RODGERS. *She stares in awe as he continues rehearsing
his song, "Sweet Candy."*

STEVE *sings with great abandon, oblivious to* DAWN, *let alone the effect
he has on her. While The Quadratics still don't sound great, under his
leadership they at least can now play in unison.*

STEVE

(*Singing*) Open up sugar, let me in!
You see I know you're momma's pearl
You're a pearl from the ocean of tears
I'm gonna steal that pearl that she don't see
Won't you give me some sweet candy

Let's get a little wild
Let's get a little crazy
Open up sugar, let me in . . .

DISSOLVE TO:

INT. DAWN'S BEDROOM—NIGHT

DAWN *lies awake in bed. She imagines hearing* STEVE *singing.*

STEVE

. . . I'm taking candy from my baby
Sweet candy from my baby.

INT. MRS. GRISSOM'S CLASS—DAY

DAWN *stands before her class with a crumpled piece of paper in her shaking hands. This is her first oral presentation, and she is miserable.*

> DAWN
>
> (*Reading*) "Dignity." Dignity is an important quality everyone should have.

> MRS. GRISSOM
>
> Louder.

> DAWN
>
> (*Continues*) That way, you will never grade-grub. Grade-grubbing is bad . . .

> MRS. GRISSOM
>
> I said louder!

> DAWN
>
> . . . because it means you're asking for a grade you shouldn't get because if you got it it wouldn't be fair to everyone else in class who didn't grade-grub.

> MRS. GRISSOM
>
> We can't hear you!

> DAWN
>
> . . . It doesn't matter whether you're a girl or boy, man or child, rich or poor, fat or thin, y-you should never be a grade-grubber. Therefore dignity is a good quality everyone should have . . .

INT. SCHOOL AUDITORIUM—DAY

Polite applause for MARY ELLEN MORIARTY, *a charismatic fifteen-year-old girl, all grace and sensitivity, who is standing at the podium about to speak to the student body.*

> MARY ELLEN
>
> Thank you.
>
> I am here to talk to you today about the dangers of talking to strangers, for I, Mary Ellen Moriarty, once talked to strangers, and that is how I became the innocent victim of a brutal kidnapping.

A hush runs through the audience. The students are riveted and remain so throughout her speech. There are exceptions, however: BRANDON, *armed with a bunch of straws, is shooting paper pellets at* DAWN, *who is sitting right in front of him.* JED *and* LANCE *muffle their laughter.* LOLITA *smirks.*

As MARY ELLEN *continues, she finds it more and more difficult to remain poised, so overcome with emotion is she.*

> MARY ELLEN
>
> Almost one year ago I was a carefree teenager, memorizing my lines for *Hello, Dolly*—I was supposed to play Dolly—(*Holds back the tears*) when one day, a day that I will never forget, I was walking home from rehearsal—I had missed my carpool—and I was waiting at the streetcorner for the light to change, when all of a sudden a dark car pulled up beside me and a big man stepped out . . . and he was older . . . and he was good-looking . . . and um . . . and he had a tattoo on his chest . . . and then the next thing I know he . . . um . . . (*Gets control of herself*) So students, I am telling you this story—

DAWN, *having decided to fight back, shoots a pellet of her own at* BRANDON. *Unfortunately, she misses and hits a teacher,* MRS. IANNONE, *instead.* MRS. IANNONE *covers her eye, shrieking in pain, thus putting an end to* MARY ELLEN's *speech.*

INT. PRINCIPAL'S OFFICE—DAY

DAWN *and her parents, tight with tension, sit opposite* MR. EDWARDS, *the principal. He has a folder open on his desk.*

> MR. EDWARDS
>
> Now what exactly did you do, Dawn?

DAWN *does not respond.*

> MRS. WIENER
>
> Dawn.

> DAWN
>
> (*Mumbles*) I shot a spitball.

> MR. EDWARDS
>
> Speak up. I can't hear you.

20

                    DAWN
I shot a spitball.

                    MRS. WIENER
You shot a what?

                    MR. WIENER
She shot a spitball.

                    MR. EDWARDS
A teacher was almost blinded.

                    DAWN
I was fighting back.

                    MRS. WIENER
Whoever told you to fight back?

A beat, then MR. WIENER *groans.*

                    MR. EDWARDS
Dawn, are you having social problems?

                DAWN / MRS. WIENER
No. / Yes.

                    MRS. WIENER
She's got no friends.

                    DAWN
I've got friends!

                    MRS. WIENER
Who?

                    DAWN
. . . Ralphy . . .

                    MRS. WIENER
Case closed. (*A beat*) She's a loner.

Through the window behind MR. EDWARDS *some kids can be seen giving the finger.*

                    MR. EDWARDS
Well, Dawn. Let me put it to you straight. We're not here to
"get" you. But you've got to understand: you're in junior high

21

now. This goes in the computer on your record. Another couple of years and this kind of incident goes on your college transcript. Any questions?

INT. SCHOOL—DAY

DAWN *and her parents walk to the parking lot in silence. They pass by* MRS. IANNONE, *now wearing a bandage over her eye.*

INT. DAWN AND MISSY'S BEDROOM—EVENING

DAWN *is lying on her bed, doing some homework;* MISSY *is playing on hers with her dolls, one of which she now discovers has been decapitated.*

> MISSY
> Were you playing with my dolls?

> DAWN
> No.

The doorbell rings.

INT. WIENER HOUSE—EVENING

MARK *opens the door and lets* STEVE *in.*

> STEVE
> Hey.

> MARK
> Hey, how's it going?

> STEVE
> Okay.

> MARK
> How come you got here so late?

> STEVE
> I dunno. Am I late?

> MARK
> Well, never mind. Come on in.

MARK *leads him up the stairs.*

> MARK
>
> Is that your computer science notebook?

> STEVE
>
> What?

> MARK
>
> Is that your computer science notebook?

> STEVE
>
> Yeah.

MARK *lets* STEVE *into his room and closes the door behind him.*

DAWN *opens her door and strains listening in to the faint talk between* MARK *and* STEVE *in* MARK*'s bedroom.*

> MARK (O.S.)
>
> I'll be right back.

DAWN *hides as* MARK *opens his bedroom door and goes to the bathroom down the hall. The coast clear, she reappears and cautiously enters* MARK*'s bedroom, where* STEVE *is now lounging atop* MARK*'s bed, listening to his walkman play "Welcome to the Dollhouse."*

DAWN *stands nervously across from* STEVE*, who is unaware of her presence. Finally, when his song ends, he looks up and notices her.*

> STEVE
>
> Oh, hey. Are you Mark's sister?

> DAWN
>
> Yeah.

Pause.

> STEVE
>
> You in junior high?

> DAWN
>
> Yeah.

> STEVE
>
> Ben Frank?

23

DAWN

Yeah.

STEVE

You like it?

DAWN

. . . No.

STEVE

Yeah, Ben Frank's pretty bad.

DAWN

You went there, too?

STEVE

Oh, yeah. I was almost expelled.

DAWN

Really? Why?

STEVE

I hated it.

DAWN

Oh, God. Me, too.

STEVE

Well, don't worry. It's only three years.

DAWN *daringly reaches out with her hand to touch his leg.*

DAWN

. . . Steve . . .

The toilet flushes o.s. and MARK *returns. On seeing* DAWN*:*

MARK

Out.

DAWN *obediently exits.* MARK *closes his door.* DAWN *leans against it, a dreamy cast to her eyes.*

MARK (O.S.)

So did you get started on the chapter?

24

STEVE (O.S.)

No.

MARK (O.S.)

'Cause it's, like, real important you focus on it if you want to get . . .

EXT. WIENER HOME—DAY

MISSY, *again in her tutu, is dancing out front by the sprinkler.*

INT. MARK'S BEDROOM—DAY

MARK *is sitting in front of his computer, but he is reading a letter from his girlfriend* NAOMI.

NAOMI (V.O.)

Dear Mark,

I've thought long and hard over what we "discussed" at camp, and talked about it with my mother. She agrees with me: sex is an important thing to experiment with before marriage, but only if there is a serious commitment on both ends.

This is my third letter to you and I am going to assume that you do not want to continue our relationship if I do not hear back from you within ten days.

Sincerely,

Your (ex-?)girlfriend,

Naomi Hayes-Blatt

p.s. I'm getting hooked up to e-mail for my birthday. I'll let you know my address as soon as it happens.

DAWN *knocks and enters, tentatively.*

DAWN

Mark?

MARK

(*Quickly stashing the letter back in his desk drawer*) Yeah?

DAWN

What are you doing?

MARK

Computer science.

DAWN

Is Steve good at computer science?

MARK

He's fair. I mean, he's definitely in the bottom quarter of the class, but he doesn't fail or anything.

DAWN

Why do you think that is?

MARK

Simple: 'cause he's lazy. All he ever thinks about is girls.

DAWN

Do you think about girls?

MARK

What, are you kidding? I want to get into a good school. My

Mark in his bedroom

future's, like, important. And besides, none of the girls at school are that pretty anyway.

DAWN

What about Maria Esposito?

MARK

Ew. Gross.

DAWN

Steve went out with her once, didn't he?

MARK

Yeah, well, Steve is horny.

DAWN

Really? How horny?

MARK

I mean, like, he'd go out with anyone as long as it was a girl and willing.

DAWN

Willing to what, *exactly*?

MARK

Go all the way.

DAWN

You mean . . . have intercourse?

MARK

Uh-duh.

DAWN

Huh.

MARK

Why, are you in love with him or something?

DAWN

No. (*Pause*) But Mark, when you say he'd go out with any girl as long as they're willing to go all the way, does that mean they also have to be pretty?

27

                              MARK
You know Tammy Steinfeld? From carpool?

                              DAWN
Yeah?

                              MARK
Okay. Do you think she's pretty?

                              DAWN
Not that pretty, really.

                              MARK
Dawn, she's a dog. And he did it with her.

                              DAWN
(*Waits a beat*) Has he ever done it with anyone younger than
high school?

                              MARK
You know Ginger Friedman?

                              DAWN
She used to be in my gym class!

                              MARK
Well, why not ask her about Steve?

EXT. 7-11—DAY

DAWN *stands in the parking lot looking toward where all the town hoods
and greasers are hanging out. She sees* GINGER, *her trampy classmate, sitting on a parked car and making out with a twentysomething biker* DUDE.

The DUDE *leaves* GINGER *for a bit to replenish the beer supply.*

                              DUDE
Be back in a second, babe. Don't move.

DAWN *walks up to* GINGER.

                              DAWN
Umm . . . Ginger? Can I talk to you for a second?

GINGER *looks up from where she is sunbathing atop a car hood.*

28

It's about Steve Rodgers.

GINGER *tenses.*

GINGER

We gotta talk.

GINGER *then rises and leads* DAWN *over to a more private area.*

GINGER

So what do you know about me and Steve?

DAWN

Well—

GINGER

First tell me who told you I knew him.

DAWN

My brother.

GINGER

Who's your brother?

DAWN

Mark Wiener.

GINGER

Him?! He's King of the Nerds!

DAWN

I know. But see, he told me you used to go out with Steve. . . .
Is it true?

GINGER

We finger fucked. Once. Last spring. That's it. It's all over now.
What else?

DAWN

Well, I was wondering if I might have a chance if he wanted to
go steady with me?

GINGER

Not a chance.

GINGER
                    DAWN
But . . .

                    GINGER
Sorry, Dawn, but that's like just the way it is. You don't cut it.

                    DAWN
What if I wore something . . . ?

                    GINGER
Dawn. Look in the mirror.

INT. BATHROOM—NIGHT

DAWN *looks at herself in the mirror. She looks at her fingers.*

                    GINGER (V.O.)
We finger fucked. Once. Last spring. That's it. It's all over now.

                    MISSY (O.S.)
What are you doing in there?

Dawn in her bathroom

None of your business!

EXT. WIENER HOME—DAY

STEVE *pulls up front, loud rock music playing from his car radio.*

INT. WIENER HOME—DAY

DAWN *is practicing piano exercises when she hears the doorbell ring. She opens the front door: it is* STEVE.

STEVE

Hey. Is Mark around?

DAWN

No. My mom took him shopping.

STEVE

Shit.

DAWN

He'll be back real soon, though, I'm pretty sure. If you want you can come inside and wait.

STEVE

(*Thinks about it a moment*) Okay. You have anything to eat?

DAWN

Yeah, follow me.

DAWN *leads* STEVE *into the kitchen. She starts opening all the food cabinets.*

DAWN

You like Yodels?

STEVE

Yeah, sure. What else you got?

DAWN

Ring Dings, Pop Tarts, Hawaiian Punch . . . whatever you want. And we've got some leftovers, too, in the fridge.

31

STEVE

Yeah, like what?

DAWN

We've got some fishsticks.

STEVE *is neither particularly impressed nor interested by what* DAWN *has
to say. He rifles through the Wieners' mail, pockets some loose change.*

STEVE

All right.

DAWN

And I know how to make Jell-O.

STEVE

Whatever.

STEVE *walks out of the kitchen and over to the living room couch. He
looks out for* MARK*'s arrival.*

DAWN (O.S.)

You know, I really like your music. (*No response*) I'm pouring
you some Hawaiian Punch. Is that all right?

STEVE

Whatever.

Now finished preparing a tray of goodies for STEVE, DAWN *enters the living room.*

DAWN

Here I come!

*She settles the tray on the coffee table and then sits demurely beside
STEVE, watching him devour the meal. Finally, after wolfing down a
half-dozen fishsticks, he licks his fingertips.*

STEVE

You not hungry?

DAWN

No.

He returns to the fishsticks.

32

DAWN

You know, I play the piano.

STEVE

Oh, yeah?

DAWN *gives* STEVE *a moment to ask her to play, but when he doesn't, she takes matters into her own hands, walks over to the piano, and begins to play.*

She fumbles valiantly through a Chopin waltz, the same one heard over the TITLE SEQUENCE.

STEVE *is still chewing fishsticks when she finishes.*

STEVE

Hey, that's pretty good.

DAWN

I could have kept going, but I sprained my finger yesterday.

STEVE

Yeah, well, you're still better than Barry any day, that's for sure.

DAWN

You think so?

STEVE

Oh, yeah. He oughta be taking lessons from you.

DAWN

Yeah, well, I don't think I have time to give lessons to Barry, but. . . . You wanna see my fingers?

STEVE

Yeah, I see 'em. (*A beat.*) Oh, shit, I gotta get going.

STEVE *rises, starts to leave.*

DAWN

Please wait. Can I play for you one more time? This time with no mistakes? Please?

The front door opens, and MISSY, MRS. WIENER, *and* MARK *appear.*

MISSY

We're home!

MRS. WIENER

We're home!

MARK

(*Seeing* STEVE) Oh, hey!

STEVE

Where were you?

DAWN *looks over toward where* STEVE *was sitting and notices something caught between the cushions: his ID card. It must have fallen out of his back pocket.* DAWN *steals it.*

MARK

Getting groceries with my mom and my sister.

STEVE

Do you know what time it is?

MARK

Yeah.

STEVE

Do you know what time you told me to be here?

MARK

What?

STEVE

I've been waiting a half an hour. What about the problems?

MARK

We'll get to them now.

STEVE

No, we won't. I've been . . .

DISSOLVE TO:

INT. CLUBHOUSE—NIGHT

DAWN *kneels in prayer at a little shrine she has built around* STEVE's *ID card. Candles illuminate it. Like a high priestess of black magic, she tries willing* STEVE *to love her.*

(*With intensity*) Steve . . . Steve . . . Steve . . . Steve . . . Steve. . . .
Hear me! You will fall in love with me. You will make love to
me. You will take me away from this place . . .

EXT. WIENER HOME—LATE AFTERNOON

The Quadratics are rehearsing. DAWN *watches, moving and eventually
singing along to the music.*

STEVE

Love's a confusing thing in my suburban home
I feel so alone
I walk through sterile rooms
There's voices in my head
A-coming from the phone

I got a blow-up doll and she looks like you
Little girl
Well the two of us have made a special world
Little girl

So welcome to the dollhouse
Welcome to the dollhouse
Welcome to the dollhouse
I got it all set up for you
Welcome to the dollhouse
Welcome to the dollhouse . . .

The song ends.

MARK

Hey, Steve, I think your singing was a little flat that time.
Barry, why don't you play an A for Steve.

BARRY *plays a note for* STEVE, *who responds with a face rigid with suppressed resentment.*

MARK

You got that, Steve?

STEVE

Fuck this shit.

And he packs up his guitar and leaves.

MARK

What's got into him?

KENNY

He can't take criticism.

MARK

Well, great. There goes the band.

DAWN *catches up with* STEVE *at the end of the driveway, by his car, while* MARK, KENNY, *and* BARRY *discuss what to do.*

STEVE

(*Muttering*) Shit.

DAWN

Wait! Wait, Steve!

STEVE

What do you want?

DAWN

You can't just go.

STEVE

Oh, why not?

DAWN

(*Searching for the answer*) . . . The band needs you!

STEVE

Tough, I quit. And you can tell your shitface brother that I'd rather fail computer science than get any more help from him.

And he gets in his car with his guitar and takes off. DAWN *watches it disappear.*

MARK, *followed by* BARRY *and* KENNY, *approach.*

MARK

I can't believe he just quit.

36

DAWN

Well, he did . . . shitface!

And she runs back inside.

MARK

(*Saving face*) She's just lucky she's a girl.

BARRY *and* KENNY *say "yeah" and nod in assent.*

EXT. 7-11—DAY

DAWN *is engrossed in a video game at the back of the store.* RALPHY *stands beside her, sipping a slurpee.*

RALPHY

Dawn. Do you think I'll get into the Hummingbirds next year?

DAWN

Boys always get in.

Pause.

RALPHY

You think they'll go on a trip to Disney World next year also?

BRANDON, JED, *and* LANCE *enter, unseen by* DAWN *and* RALPHY. *They stroll down by the magazine section, shoplifting.*

DAWN

I don't know. Maybe. It depends.

RALPHY

On what—?

The bullies have spotted some prey.

BRANDON

Hey, dogface!

The bullies approach, cornering them.

DAWN

Drop dead.

37

RALPHY

Let's go.

BRANDON

What's the matter, faggot? In a hurry to run home to mommy?

DAWN

Shut up.

BRANDON

Make me, lesbo.

DAWN

You think you're so cool.

RALPHY

You think you're hot shit, but you're really just cold diarrhea.

BRANDON, JED, *and* LANCE *crack up.*

BRANDON

Listen to this faggot!

DAWN

Shut up, you assholes.

RALPHY

Yeah, shut up.

BRANDON

Man, if I were you, faggot, I'd be shitting in my pants, 'cause when you go to Junior High, man . . . I'm gonna smash that little fairy face of yours into a mushy pulp.

DAWN

Yeah, well, at least he won't stay back a year.

BRANDON *knocks* DAWN*'s slurpee out of her hand.* BRANDON, JED, *and* LANCE *crack up yet again.*

DAWN

(*To* BRANDON) Retard.

And DAWN, *followed by* RALPHY, *stalks off.*

BRANDON, JED, *and* LANCE *have stopped laughing. The feeling is ominous.*

EXT. SCHOOL—MORNING

A bright day at the "penitentiary."

INT. SCHOOL HALLWAY—DAY

DAWN hums Steve Rodgers' "Sweet Candy" to herself as she looks for something in her locker.

>   BRANDON
> Hey, Wiener.

>   DAWN
> Whadya want?

>   BRANDON
> You better get ready. 'Cause at three o'clock today . . . I'm
> gonna rape you.

INT. MATH CLASS—DAY

Several students stand up by the blackboard and solve equations for the class. DAWN is one of these students, and so is BRANDON. When the MATH TEACHER isn't looking, BRANDON gestures threateningly at DAWN with his chalk.

DOOMSDAY MUSIC throbs on the soundtrack.

INT. SCIENCE CLASS—DAY

DAWN sits frozen with fear in lab attire while her SCIENCE TEACHER explains something to her. Walking right behind the TEACHER is BRANDON, now wielding some bunsen burner hose.

INT. HALLWAY—DAY

An automaton-like DAWN walks along, now accompanied by a chattering girlfriend. Only DAWN notices BRANDON as they pass right by him, now licking a knife.

39

INT. SCHOOL LIBRARY—DAY

DAWN *sits at a carrel in a remote corner of the room. She looks around: the clock reads just a minute before three. She lifts her head cautiously and suddenly sees* BRANDON. *He is standing across the room from her, in the stacks, eying her, waiting.* DAWN *ducks her head, terrified. But then she looks up again, this time noticing* LOLITA *as she sashays over toward* BRANDON *from behind.* DAWN *follows their faint dialogue:*

> LOLITA
>
> Forget that ugly bitch.

> BRANDON
>
> Bug off.

> LOLITA
>
> You comin' over to my house tonight?

> BRANDON
>
> Get the fuck away from me, okay?

> LOLITA
>
> (*Seductively*) Aw, come on . . .

The three o'clock bell rings. Students rise from their desks to leave. BRANDON, *rejecting* LOLITA*'s advances, shoves her away. He passes by* DAWN, *menacingly, then stalks off.*

EXT. SCHOOL—DAY

Students rush out to the buses and carpools.

BACK TO THE LIBRARY—DAY

Thinking it now safe, DAWN *packs up her stuff and heads off as well, only in the opposite direction.*

INT. SCHOOL HALLWAY—DAY

It is dark and abandoned. DAWN *appears, looks behind her, and heads for the side exit.*

EXT. SCHOOL SIDE EXIT—DAY

Just as she thinks she is free a hand shoots out from around the corner and grabs her. The hand belongs to BRANDON. *He swings her around and pushes her up against the wall, next to a dumpster.*

> BRANDON

Nice try, bitch.

> DAWN

No, no . . . I was trying to meet you . . .

> BRANDON

Don't bullshit me, you piece of ugly fuck.

> DAWN

I-I'm sorry.

> BRANDON

Sorry for shit. (*Presses hard on* DAWN*'s wrist*) So you still think I'm a retard?

> DAWN

No, Brandon! You're not a retard. . . . Please stop. . . . You're hurting me! . . .

The two of them stand opposite one another, panting. For a while they say and do nothing, just staring at each other. Then BRANDON *pulls out a knife.*

> BRANDON

Now strip.

But DAWN *does nothing.*

> BRANDON

Strip!

Still she just stands there.

Suddenly the door is heard opening and the JANITOR *appears with some garbage for the dumpster.*

DAWN *leaps free and runs off, disappearing in a flash.*

BRANDON

Bitch.

INT. WIENER HOME—DAY

MARK, MISSY, *and* MRS. WIENER *are seated on the living room sofa around the coffee table. They are making party preparations.*

MRS. WIENER

Now listen. When your sister gets here let me do most of the talking, all right? But back me up whatever.

DAWN *appears from the kitchen.*

MRS. WIENER

Oh, Dawn! Come join us. We need your help.

DAWN *stays where she is, suspicious.*

MISSY

We're having a party!

DAWN

What for?

MARK

Mom and Dad's twentieth, dinghead.

MRS. WIENER

(*Reproving*) Mark. (*To* DAWN) I was talking with your dad, and we thought it would be a great idea if this year we celebrated our anniversary in the backyard. We could set up tables and there'd be dancing and Mark's band is gonna be the music. Your brother has even promised to write a song special for us. It's our twentieth, you know. So what do you think if we all pitch in together?

DAWN

Okay.

MISSY

Mom wants you to tear down your clubhouse.

But that's the Special People Club!

MRS. WIENER

(*Rising*) Oh, honey, I know. But we really need the space. And besides, it's not really very pretty, is it? And you're getting a little old for clubhouses . . .

The telephone rings. MRS. WIENER *gets it.*

MRS. WIENER

Hello. . . . Whom may I say is calling, please? . . . Certainly, hold on a moment. Dawn? It's for you.

DAWN

(*Into receiver*) Hello?

We cut back and forth now between BRANDON *in extreme close-up at his place and* DAWN.

BRANDON

Hey, ugly.

Brandon sets a date for rape

DAWN

(*Tries to control a sudden trembling*) O-oh, hi.

BRANDON

Why'd you hurry off like that?

DAWN

I-I was in a rush.

BRANDON

The fuck you were.

DAWN

R-really, I—

BRANDON

Tomorrow. Same time. Same place. You get raped. (*Pause*) Be there.

BRANDON *hangs up.*

DAWN *is weak with fear, but doesn't let on. Her mother and* MISSY *calmly and cheerfully go about their party planning in the background.*

MRS. WIENER

So? Who is this Brandon?

DAWN

Just this kid from school.

MRS. WIENER

Is he a nice boy?

DAWN

Yeah, he's okay.

EXT. BENJAMIN FRANKLIN JUNIOR HIGH—DAY

It's three o'clock. The students come bursting outside.

EXT. SCHOOL SIDE EXIT—DAY

BRANDON *leans against the wall, smoking.*

DAWN *comes out, like a sheep to slaughter.*

44

BRANDON

You alone?

DAWN

Yeah.

BRANDON

What time do you have to be home by?

DAWN

Four-thirty.

DAWN *starts unbuttoning her blouse.*

BRANDON

Wait. I have something I want you to do for me first. Come on.
This way. (*Brandishing his knife*) And don't try anything stupid.

And he leads her away.

EXT. AN ABANDONED SITE—DAY

BRANDON *walks* DAWN *over to a make-out point. He sits down on a
rock, she on a torn mattress.*

DAWN

Do you want me to lie down?

BRANDON

Okay.

DAWN *lies down.* BRANDON *lights up.*

BRANDON

You wanna smoke first?

DAWN

(*Acting casual*) No, thanks.

BRANDON

Afraid?

DAWN

No. I just don't feel like it. (*Pause, watches him smoke*) But I
think marijuana should be legalized.

45

BRANDON

Why do you always have to be such a cunt?

BRANDON *walks over to the wire fence. His back is to* DAWN.

DAWN

(*Taken by surprise, perplexed*) I'm sorry. (*No response*)
Brandon . . . I don't mean to be a cunt.

Pause.

BRANDON

You know I've got a brother?

DAWN

No. I never knew that. What grade's he in?

BRANDON

He's not in any grade. He's retarded.

DAWN

Oh.

DAWN *rises, starts walking over toward* BRANDON.

Dawn and Brandon consider rape

I'm sorry.

BRANDON

There's nothing to be sorry about. He's a tough kid. He could beat you up if he wanted.

DAWN

I'm sorry—I mean . . . yeah.

BRANDON *kisses her.* DAWN *is stiff with fear. He kisses her again.*

DAWN

Brandon . . . are you still going to rape me?

BRANDON

What time is it?

DAWN

I dunno. But I guess I don't have to be home yet.

BRANDON

Nah, there's not enough time.

DAWN

Thanks, Brandon.

BRANDON

Yeah, but just remember: this didn't happen. I mean, no one . . . *Fucking no one . . .*

DAWN

I swear I won't tell anybody. Not a soul.

BRANDON

'Cause if you do, I really will rape you next time.

DAWN

Okay.

INT. WIENER HOME—EVENING

All the Wieners are at the dining room table. MRS. WIENER *has begun clearing the food.*

MRS. WIENER

You know, I have to tell you. I'm very upset with you three.

MISSY

But Mommy, I didn't do anything wrong.

MRS. WIENER

I know, just Mark and Dawn.

MARK

But Mom, I already spoke to Steve.

MRS. WIENER

And did you apologize?

MARK

Yes. I just had to promise to give him two hundred dollars for playing at your party.

MR. WIENER

Two hundred dollars!

MRS. WIENER

Oh, for Chrissake, Harv. It's our twentieth!

MARK

Well, in any case, he's coming by later to go over some stuff with me. There's a big computer science test tomorrow.

MRS. WIENER

And what about you, Dawn? Are you going to tear down that mess in the backyard or not? (*No response.*) Dawn, I am talking to you.

DAWN

No.

MR. WIENER

Dawn, listen to your mom and forget about it.

DAWN

No. The clubhouse stands and that's final.

MRS. WIENER

(*With suppressed anger*) Fine. Have it your way.

48

                    MR. WIENER
Dawn, be smart. Make things easy on yourself.

                        DAWN
No.

MRS. WIENER *and* MISSY *carry in plates of scrumptious chocolate cake to the table.*

                    MR. WIENER
Mmm. Now this I like.

                        MARK
Yeah. Where did you get it?

                    MRS. WIENER
The supermarket.

                        MISSY
I picked it out.

MRS. WIENER *decides not to give* DAWN *a piece of cake.* DAWN *watches her family devour the dessert, the lone upright, unserved slice of cake staring her in the face.*

                        MISSY
(*While still working on her first piece of cake*) Mom, since Dawn isn't eating hers, can me and Mark split it?

                        MARK
(*Mouth full of cake*) Yeah, can we?

                        MISSY
Please?

MRS. WIENER *looks over at* DAWN, *but she just keeps her eyes on the extra cake slice, her face set rigid with determination.* MRS. WIENER *decides to give* DAWN*'s piece of cake to* MARK *and* MISSY.

                    MRS. WIENER
Go ahead.

DAWN *continues staring at the spot where the cake once stood while her siblings demolish the last piece of it.*

                              MRS. WIENER
Mark. Missy. I'm gonna need your help this weekend.

                                MARK
What do we have to do?

                              MRS. WIENER
Tear down that mess in the backyard.

FADE TO BLACK.

INT. MARK'S ROOM—EVENING

DAWN *and* STEVE *lie on the bed together, examining a recently developed*
batch of snapshots. The photos are all of STEVE.

                                STEVE
Whadya think?

                                DAWN
I think . . . oh, Steve. They're all so beautiful.

                                STEVE
They're from the summer.

                                DAWN
Who took them?

                                STEVE
Valerie Mondello. She's photo editor of the yearbook.

                                DAWN
Was she your girlfriend?

                                STEVE
For a few days. It was worth it, though, don't you think?

                                DAWN
Oh, yes.

                                STEVE
I'm thinking of using this one for my first album cover . . .

                                DAWN
You're going to be on a record?

                                 50

STEVE

It'll happen. It's gotta happen. It's just a question of time.

DAWN

You think before graduation?

STEVE

Fuck graduation.

DAWN

What about college?

STEVE

Fuck college. I'm just doing this computer science shit with Mark for my parents. As soon as I make enough money I'm moving into the city. That's where it's all happening.

DAWN

Oh.

MARK *enters with a computer diskette in hand.*

MARK

I found the disc! (*Noticing* DAWN) Out.

DAWN

No.

MARK

Whadya mean no? I said out.

DAWN

No. Steve and I are talking.

MARK

Come on, I said out. Come on!

He tries using force, but she resists.

MARK

(*Calling out to the hallway*) MOMMMM!

STEVE

Leave her alone.

MARK

You don't understand. This is my room.

STEVE

So what? You're being, like, a total fascist.

MRS. WIENER (o.s.)
(*Calling from afar*) What is it, Mark?!

MARK, *humiliated, looks at* DAWN, *then* STEVE. *He decides finally not to respond to his mother. Instead he returns to the computer to resume the tutorial.*

MARK

Did you solve any of the problems?

INT. HOMEROOM CLASS—MORNING

The CAMERA *pans across the faces of bored students while an intercom relays the following message from the principal:*

Good morning, students. All Hummingbird chorus members going on the concert tour to Disney World this year must hand in signed permission slips by this Friday, the latest.

On a more worrisome note, drugs were found extinguished yesterday in the boys' lavatory. Now, I want to remind you all that any student caught using or selling drugs will be immediately expelled from school and dealt with by the police authorities. There will be no exceptions.

Drugs are illegal: Just say no.

Thank you for your attention.

Pretty and popular COOKIE *raises her hand. The teacher is* MRS. IANNONE, *who now wears a black eye-patch.*

COOKIE

Mrs. Iannone?

MRS. IANNONE

Yes, Cookie?

I have an announcement.

MRS. IANNONE

Go ahead.

COOKIE

(*She rises.*) For everyone coming to my birthday party: remember to bring along a bathing suit. (*To* MRS. IANNONE) That's all.

INT. HALLWAY—DAY

DAWN, *standing by her open locker, observes the following scene:*

COOKIE *is taking some gift-wrapped presents out of her festively decorated locker and showing them off to a small group of envious and admiring girlfriends. They all giggle and chatter (i.e., "Oh, my God! . . .")*

But then BRANDON *appears. Gruffly but shyly he approaches* COOKIE. *Everyone is silent.*

Dawn and her locker

53

BRANDON

Hey, Cookie.

COOKIE

What do you want?

BRANDON

How come I wasn't invited? Jed and Lance were.

COOKIE

Oh, well, I really would have, Brandon, but we needed an even number of girls and boys, and if you were invited there would be too many boys.

BRANDON

Well, I got something for you.

COOKIE

What is it?

BRANDON

Open it up.

BRANDON *hands her a little package clumsily scotch-taped together with paper napkins.* COOKIE *opens it up and finds a giant, but broken, chocolate chip cookie inside.*

BRANDON

I didn't eat my dessert at lunch today. I saved it for you. Now can I come to your birthday party this weekend?

COOKIE

But Brandon . . . this didn't even cost anything.

And COOKIE, *escorted by her tittering friends, walks away.*

BRANDON *remains fixed to his spot. But then he notices* DAWN *and realizes she has been watching him the whole time. She stands still.* BRANDON *walks toward her and then stops in front of her, full of anger and menace.*

BRANDON

What are you looking at?

DAWN

Nothing.

54

He smashes her locker in with his fist. Then he walks away, DAWN *staring after him.*

EXT. SKY—NIGHT

A shot of the moon floating through the clouds.

INT. DAWN'S CLUBHOUSE—NIGHT

DAWN *and* BRANDON *lie on a blanket on the ground. They listen to a tape play in a portable cassette deck: "Lost in Your Eyes," a romantic ballad by Debbie Gibson.*

> BRANDON
>
> Sorry about your locker.

> DAWN
>
> Oh, it's okay. I mean, it's not really mine anyway. It's the school's.

Pause.

> BRANDON
>
> Anyway, I hate those stupid kinds of parties. They always treat you like little kids. She probably had a fucking magician.

> DAWN
>
> Yeah. I hate parties, too. (*Pause*) My parents are tearing this down tomorrow.

> BRANDON
>
> Fuck. What for?

> DAWN
>
> Their anniversary.

> BRANDON
>
> Assholes.

The tape ends.

> BRANDON
>
> Where'd you get that cassette player?

> DAWN
>
> Ralphy gave it to me.

55

BRANDON

Why do you hang out with that faggot?

DAWN

Ralphy?

BRANDON

Yeah.

DAWN

Just because he's a faggot doesn't mean he's an asshole.

BRANDON

(*Thinks this over*) Yeah, maybe.

BRANDON *starts kissing her.*

DAWN

Brandon, I can't be your girlfriend.

BRANDON

Huh?

DAWN

I want to but . . . I'm in love with someone else.

BRANDON

Who?

DAWN

You wouldn't know him.

BRANDON

What's his name?

DAWN

It's no one you know.

BRANDON

What's his name?

DAWN

He's older.

BRANDON

What's his fucking name?!!!

> DAWN

Steve Rodgers. He's in high school. Brandon . . . Brandon . . .

She tries touching him, but he flinches. He gets up, stalks off.

EXT. CLUBHOUSE—NIGHT

DAWN *tries catching up with* BRANDON.

> DAWN

Brandon, wait! Where're you going? We still have some Yodels left!

She tries grabbing him, but he just throws her to the ground.

> BRANDON

Asshole.

DAWN *cries.*

RALPHY, *hidden behind a hedge, has been watching* DAWN *and* BRANDON *and their entire drama unfolding the whole time.* BRANDON *gone, he now emerges to comfort* DAWN.

> RALPHY

Don't feel bad, Dawn. Brandon McCarthy's just a retard.

> DAWN

. . . Faggot!

And she hurries into her house.

EXT. WIENER BACKYARD—DAY

PARTY-TIME!

It is a beautiful sunny day. The CAMERA TILTS UP *from* MR. AND MRS. WIENER'*s Twentieth-Anniversary cake to the happy couple,* MISSY, *and their friends, among whom are* MR. AND MRS. KASDAN.

STEVE, *backed up by the Quadratics, sings the song* MARK *wrote:*

> STEVE

It was twenty years ago today
When Harv and Marj were married

There were three little twinkles in their eyes
When over the threshold Marj was carried . . .

Everyone starts dancing, clapping, laughing, etc.

MISSY *does some ballet solos until* MR. KASDAN *lifts her up onto his shoulders and starts dancing.*

> STEVE
>
> Harv and Marj, you're the greatest
> You're the greatest couple the world has ever seen
> We love you both, we wish you the best
> Happy anniversary, great joy and happiness
>
> Happy anniversary! Happy anniversary to you!
> Happy anniversary! Happy anniversary to you!
>
> You're the king of the breadwinners, Harv
> And Marj, you're the queen of mothers
> Missy, Mark, and Dawn
> Are your lucky son and daughters

MR. AND MRS. WIENER *now notice that* DAWN *is missing.*

> MR. WIENER
>
> Where's Dawn?

> MRS. WIENER
>
> I don't know. Where is . . . ? (*To* MRS. KASDAN) Rita, did you see Dawn?

> STEVE
>
> Happy anniversary! Happy anniversary to you!
> Happy anniversary! Happy anniversary to you!

The song ends as the CAMERA *finds* DAWN *staring balefully out the window.*

INT. WIENER HOME—DAY

DAWN *watches as the band and dancers take a break. She sees* MISSY *flirting with* STEVE *as he lifts her up into his arms to give her a whirl. She overhears:*

58

STEVE

How are you?

MISSY

I'm fine.

STEVE

Yeah? . . .

DAWN *turns away from the window, bitter and furious. She has dressed herself up to be "sexy" like Ginger Friedman, but it's not really working.*

EXT. WIENER BACKYARD—DAY

DAWN *comes outside. There is purpose to her gait. She interrupts her parents, who are in the midst of chatting with some guests.*

DAWN

Where's Steve?

MR. WIENER

Hey, look who's here!

MRS. WIENER

Where have you been?

DAWN

Leave me alone. I'm looking for Steve.

She sees MARK *at the bandstand and approaches him.*

DAWN

Where's Steve?

MARK

I don't know. Leave me alone. I'm trying to figure something out.

DAWN *looks around, goes over to* MISSY.

DAWN

Where's Steve?

MISSY

(*Pointing*) In the garage.

DAWN *goes there and knocks on the door.*

59

Dawn dolled up for Steve at her parents' anniversary party

Steve! Open up! Open up!

The door opens partway. STEVE *appears.*

Hey, Dawn! What's up?

I have to talk to you.

What about?

I was wondering if—

DAWN *hesitates as* STEVE's BEAUTIFUL GIRLFRIEND *now appears beside him.*

W-well, I've been thinking seriously of building another club-house and well . . . I wanted to know . . . would you be interested in being my first honorary member?

Steve and his girlfriend

                          STEVE
What? What are you talking about?

                          DAWN
The Special People Club.

                          STEVE
Special People?

STEVE *makes a face.*

                          DAWN
What's the matter?

                          STEVE
Do you know what Special People means?

                          DAWN
What?

                          STEVE
Special People equals retarded. Your club is for retards.

STEVE *shuts the door on* DAWN, *who remains standing, rooted to the spot, immobile.*

INT. TV ROOM—NIGHT

The tape of the anniversary party is playing on the TV.

The entire WIENER FAMILY *is watching the home movie. Thrills of joy and laughter, except, of course, from* DAWN.

                       MISSY (O.S.)
Hey, Mommy! Look!

The TV shows footage of MISSY *performing pirouettes for the party guests.*

                    MRS. WIENER (O.S.)
I see, honey! Oh! Oh, look at Missy! Oh, God, you are so cute!!

The TV now shows footage of MISSY *riding* MR. KASDAN *piggy-back as he dances.*

                    MRS. WIENER (O.S.)
Oh! Look at her dancing with Mr. Kasdan!

The TV now shows STEVE *giving* MISSY *an "airplane" ride.*

MISSY (O.S.)
And look at me and Steve! Steve really likes me.

And now some close-up footage of MARK *playing the clarinet.*

MARK (O.S.)
Hey, I look pretty good there!

MR. WIENER (O.S.)
And you sound good, too!

MRS. WIENER (O.S.)
Oh, Harv. We have to get copies of this tape.

MARK (O.S.)
Yeah. Unfortunately Steve just quit the band.

MR. AND MRS. WIENER
What?!

MR. WIENER
I just gave him two hundred dollars!

MRS. WIENER
And didn't you just tell me that he got an A on his computer science final?

MARK
Well, it's not that. He dropped out of school and left town. He wants to try making it in New York as the next Jim Morrison.

MR. WIENER
Stupid idiot kid. He'll never make it.

MARK
Yeah, that's what I told him. He'll never get into a good school now.

MRS. WIENER
No, he won't make it . . .

MR. WIENER
Never make it . . .

MRS. WIENER

Never . . .

Pause.

Their attention returns to the home movie video tape: DAWN *is now standing by the kiddie pool.* MISSY *pushes her in the water. The tape ends.*

Everyone (except DAWN*) has a good laugh.*

MISSY

Mommy! Let's watch it again!

INT. WIENER HOME—NIGHT

All is quiet.

INT. DAWN'S BEDROOM—NIGHT

DAWN *rises from bed. She has a hammer in her hand. She walks over to* MISSY*'s bed: her sister is asleep. Then, as quietly as possible, she sneaks out to . . .*

INT. THE HALLWAY—NIGHT

DAWN *continues to tread carefully lest she wake anyone up. She tiptoes down the stairs.*

INT. TV ROOM—NIGHT

DAWN *enters the room and goes straight for the VCR. She presses the eject button. A video cassette pops out.*

EXT. WIENER HOME—NIGHT

DAWN *hurries out to the front, where the party trash is tied up neatly in black plastic bags. She sets the cassette down on the ground and gives it three big whacks with her hammer.*

INT. DAWN'S BEDROOM—NIGHT

DAWN *returns to her room. She pauses for a moment as she looks over at* MISSY, *back at her hammer, and then back at* MISSY *again. She tiptoes over to* MISSY *to the point where she is hovering over her, feeling her little breaths blow gently against her.* DAWN *lifts the hammer and then just stands in this life-threatening position, tense and anguished, for a few moments. Finally she relaxes, returns to her bed, and puts the hammer back under the pillow.*

DAWN

You're so lucky.

INT. SCHOOL HALLWAY—DAY

The bell rings and students flood the hallway.

DAWN *is putting some books away in her locker when she happens to see* BRANDON *walking by. He pretends she doesn't exist. She stares after him, a look of pain and yearning on her face.*

INT. MRS. GRISSOM'S CLASS—DAY

Another test in progress. DAWN *tosses* BRANDON *a note. He flicks it off his desk, not even looking her way.*

The classroom door suddenly opens and MR. EDWARDS *appears,* TWO POLICEMEN *hovering behind in the doorway.* MRS. GRISSOM *walks over to him.*

MR. EDWARDS

Would you ask Brandon McCarthy to step outside, please?

MRS. GRISSOM

Is something wrong?

MR. EDWARDS

The police want to ask him a few questions.

MRS. GRISSOM

Brandon, come up here, please.

BRANDON *rises with his test.*

65

MRS. GRISSOM

You can leave your test.

He passes DAWN, *still not even glancing at her.*

MR. EDWARDS

Come along, Brandon. Thank you, Martha. Sorry for the interruption.

BRANDON *leaves the classroom, escorted by* MR. EDWARDS *and the* TWO POLICEMEN.

EXT. SIDEWALK BY THE WIENER HOME—DAY

Little children play in the street. DAWN *trudges along, downcast. She smacks a ball out of a* LITTLE BOY's *hands.*

She arrives at her driveway just as MRS. WIENER *is pulling out in the station wagon.*

MRS. WIENER

(*Braking*) Oh, Dawn! Oh, I'm so glad I caught you. Listen now, Dad just called. His car broke down and I have to go pick him up at the car dealer. Now I've left a note in the kitchen for Missy to give to Mrs. Golden, but in case she doesn't see it when she gets in be sure to tell her to get a ride home from ballet with her. I won't be able to pick her up like I told her I would. Okay?

DAWN

Yeah.

MRS. WIENER

Now, you won't forget?

DAWN

No.

INT. WIENER HOME—DAY

DAWN *comes inside and immediately notices the note her mother left for* MISSY. *She picks it up, reads it, and then brings it into the TV room with a glass of soda. She climbs on the sofa and flicks on the TV.*

. . . And that means hungry for love. They haven't gotten
enough love. They haven't gotten enough affection. They
haven't gotten enough attention from their partner or from the
people in their life. See, I like to think of your relationship as a
living breathing thing, and I have found . . .

The telephone starts ringing. DAWN *does nothing. She hears* MISSY *fumbling with the key to the front door, and still does nothing. Finally* MISSY *comes running inside.*

MISSY

I'll get it! (*Picking up the phone*) Wiener residence. Whom may I
ask is calling, please? . . . (*To* DAWN) It's Ralphy.

DAWN

Tell him I'm punished.

MISSY

But you're not punished.

DAWN

Well, I don't feel like talking to him.

MISSY

But he's your friend. So here.

MISSY *tries handing* DAWN *the phone, but she won't take it.*

MISSY

Dawwwn.

INT. RALPHY'S BEDROOM

RALPHY *listens on the telephone to the following exchange:*

DAWN (O.S.)

Hang it up. I don't want to speak to that faggot.

MISSY (O.S.)

But Dawn . . .

DAWN (O.S.)

Hang it up!

67

MISSY (O.S.)
But he's your friend.

DAWN (O.S.)
He is not. He's a spy and an asshole.

MISSY (O.S.)
But Dawn. Ralphy likes you.

DAWN (O.S.)
Yeah? Well, that's too bad, 'cause you can tell him I hope he
rots in hell.

MISSY (O.S.)
Dawn. Maybe you should say you're sorry.

DAWN (O.S.)
Fuck you!

The line goes dead.

BACK TO DAWN AND MISSY:

MISSY *returns from the kitchen with a little changing bag and stops by*
DAWN.

MISSY
You know you're not supposed to drink in the TV room.

A car horn suddenly toots from the driveway. MISSY *hurries off, but then*
DAWN, *remembering the note, calls:*

DAWN
Oh, hey, Missy!

MISSY
(*Returns*) What?

DAWN
(*Considering whether or not to give* MISSY *the note, finally*
deciding:) Nothing.

And MISSY *runs out.* DAWN *pockets the note.*

EXT. WIENER HOME—NIGHT

All the lights are on. Police cars are in the driveway. The sound of walkie-talkies.

INT. WIENER HOME—NIGHT

MARK *sits beside his weeping father, and* DAWN, *guiltily, sits beside her weeping mother.* POLICEMEN *and* DETECTIVES *review the situation. Their lines overlap:*

> POLICEMAN #1
> . . . four-feet-three inches, fifty-four pounds, long blonde hair, blue eyes, last seen wearing a pink leotard, pink ballet slippers, and pink tutu . . .

> POLICEMAN #2
> . . . Yeah . . . You copy that? . . .

> POLICEMAN #3
> . . . at six-fifteen . . .

> POLICEMAN #4
> . . . Yeah . . . No, she just claims to have given her the note . . .

> POLICEMAN #5
> . . . Her sister says she gave her the note . . .

> POLICEMAN #1
> . . . Yeah, well, she claims to have given her the note . . .

FADE TO BLACK.

INT. WIENER HOME—DAY

DAWN *and* MARK *sit at the kitchen table eating breakfast cereal.* POLICE-MEN *and* DETECTIVES *shuffle around in the background.* MRS. WIENER *is talking with some of them, answering questions.*

> MARK
> So you're not going to school today?

> DAWN
> No. Mom's afraid I'll be kidnapped also.

69

MARK

(*Sarcastic*) Yeah, right.

DAWN

(*Defensive*) What?

MARK

Never mind.

Pause. Some POLICEMEN *walk nearby.*

DAWN

What do you think they're looking around for?

MARK

Clues.

DAWN

But she's not here.

MARK

Uh-duh.

The police SERGEANT *comes to the table and sits down across from them, scribbling some notes. Finally* DAWN *works up the courage to address him:*

DAWN

Excuse me, sergeant. Do you think they'll find her?

SERGEANT

(*Moved by the sight of innocent-looking* DAWN) Are you the big sister?

DAWN

Yeah.

SERGEANT

And you're the big brother?

MARK

Yeah.

But the SERGEANT *just nods in silence without ever responding to* DAWN'*s question. He awakens at last from his melancholy reverie when* MRS. WIENER, *still dressed in her robe, returns to the kitchen to prepare*

70

some tea. He rises from the table and walks over to confer with her.
DAWN *and* MARK *lower their voices:*

> MARK
>
> You know, Dad's real sick. He's probably gonna have to go to the hospital.

> DAWN
>
> Why? What's wrong with him?

> MARK
>
> The doctor's not sure, but Mom thinks it might be a nervous breakdown. It's probably just his gallbladder.

DAWN *looks over at her mother as, hands shaking, she lifts the tea tray.*

> DAWN
>
> (*Louder, rising, with cheer*) I'll help, Mom!

> MRS. WIENER
>
> Thank you, Dawn. (*Handing her the tray*) Here, you want to take that up to your father while I talk to the police sergeant?

> DAWN
>
> Sure, Mom.

DAWN *leaves the kitchen, tray in hand.*

INT. MR. AND MRS. WIENER'S BEDROOM—DAY

DAWN *enters quietly, carefully setting the tray down beside the bed. She looks at her father. It is unclear whether he is awake or asleep. His face is sallow, sweaty.*

> DAWN
>
> Dad? . . . I brought you some tea. . . . How are you feeling? . . . Better? . . . Well, don't worry, they'll find Missy, I'm sure of it. And if they don't, well, remember: you've still got me and Mark . . .

MR. WIENER *emits a feeble groan.*

EXT. HIGHWAY/BACKROAD—DAY

DAWN *bicycles furiously to the other side of town.*

EXT. BRANDON'S HOUSE—DAY

DAWN *arrives at a ramshackle house in a run-down neighborhood. The yard is untended, a pickup in the unpaved driveway. The house hasn't been painted in ages.*

DAWN *parks her bike and walks up to the front door. She buzzes.*

The door opens. BRANDON*'s retarded brother* TOMMY *is standing there with a jelly doughnut.*

> TOMMY
> Hello. (*Offers* DAWN *the doughnut*) Wanna bite?

But DAWN *just looks dumbly at him, too fearful to move or say anything.*

> MR. MCCARTHY (O.S.)
> Tommy? Tommy!

MR. MCCARTHY *comes to the front door.*

> MR. MCCARTHY
> (*To* TOMMY) Go on. Get back in the kitchen.

TOMMY *obeys his father.*

> MR. MCCARTHY
> (*To* DAWN) Who are you?

> DAWN
> Dawn Wiener . . . I'm a friend of Brandon McCarthy.

> MR. MCCARTHY
> Whadya want?

> DAWN
> Like, I was wondering if I could see Brandon.

> MR. MCCARTHY
> How come you're not in school?

DAWN

M-my sister was kidnapped. My Mom let me stay home today.

MR. MCCARTHY

So whadya want with Brandon?

DAWN

I wanted to talk to him.

MR. MCCARTHY

Wha'd he do? Knock you up or something?

DAWN

Oh, no, no . . .

MR. MCCARTHY

(*Looks her up and down*) Okay then, go ahead, you can go say good-bye to him. Go on, up the stairs, at the back. But you got just one hour, then we're leaving.

DAWN

Thank you, Mr. McCarthy.

She goes inside, he closes the door behind her.

INT. BRANDON'S ROOM—DAY

DAWN *climbs a dark, creaky staircase. At the landing she pauses to look around, then turns to open a door:* BRANDON's *bedroom.*

The room is cramped and musty, stark and depressing. A Playboy bunny poster decorates one wall.

She sees BRANDON *folding up a sleeping bag, packing up his belongings. He doesn't look up when she enters.*

DAWN

Hi, Brandon.

BRANDON

What are you doing here?

DAWN

I tried calling you, but my mom wouldn't let me because my sister was kidnapped.

73

BRANDON

Yeah, I heard. So whadya want?

DAWN *closes the door and comes closer.*

DAWN

I want to be your girlfriend.

BRANDON

Too late. I'm leaving.

DAWN

Where're you going?

BRANDON

None of your business.

DAWN

Can I come along?

BRANDON

No.

DAWN

Are you gonna go back to school?

BRANDON

No way, man. I'm not going to no reformatory either. My dad thinks I'm going, but he can go to hell. I'm gettin' out of here.

DAWN

You mean you're running away?

BRANDON

Yup. To New York.

DAWN

Does anybody know?

BRANDON

No.

DAWN *moves to kiss him, but* BRANDON *pushes her away.*

BRANDON

Get offa me. (*But then, pulling her into an embrace:*) I'm the one that makes the first move.

74

They kiss.

BRANDON

Now, come on.

DAWN

R-right now?

BRANDON

Now or never.

DAWN

But I can't now.

BRANDON

Why not? What are you, scared?

DAWN

No, but I—

BRANDON

What?

DAWN

Can't you wait just a little longer? I mean, I'm sure Mr. Edwards
will let you back in if you stop dealing drugs.

BRANDON

Who said I deal drugs?

DAWN

But Brandon, everyone says—

Pause.

BRANDON

And you believed them all.

DAWN

You mean . . . you didn't . . . ?

BRANDON

Asshole. Jed's the one that deals. But, hey, don't feel bad.
You're like everyone else. You think I'm some lying asshole.
And you know something, Dawn? I don't give a fuck.

                              DAWN
        I believe you.

                            BRANDON
        Gee, thanks. I feel so much better.

                              DAWN
        But I really do.

                            BRANDON
        The fuck you do!

                              DAWN
        Brandon, I do!

                            BRANDON
        Lying piece of shit!

                              DAWN
        Brandon, please wait. I'm so sorry . . .

                            BRANDON
        Well, it's too late. I'm gettin' outta here. And who knows?
        Maybe I will deal drugs now.

                        MR. MCCARTHY (O.S.)
        You packed? We're leaving in ten minutes!

                            BRANDON
        Well, are you coming?

                              DAWN
        I can't.

BRANDON *jumps out the window.*

                              DAWN
        Brandon! Wait! Please don't go!

DAWN *watches from the window as* BRANDON *gets up from the ground,
gathers his stuff, and walks off.*

DISSOLVE TO:

INT. WIENER HOME—EVENING

                               76

Mark and Dawn listen for the latest info on Missy's whereabouts

MRS. WIENER, MARK, *and* DAWN *sit at the dinner table. Only* MARK *eats heartily.* MRS. WIENER *is looking tired, haggard. A telephone rests on the table, always an arm's reach away from her. For a time, nobody talks. Until:*

> MARK
>
> So how's Dad?

> MRS. WIENER
>
> They don't know yet. They're still doing more testing.

> MARK
>
> Can I visit him?

> MRS. WIENER
>
> What are you doing tomorrow after school?

> MARK
>
> Tomorrow's no good. I've got a big Forensic Society debate. But I'm sure I can get out of it.

> MRS. WIENER
>
> No, Mark. Go. I want you to. It's important . . . Dawn can

come with me to the hospital. And I'll get your Aunt Phyllis to stay by the phone.

The telephone rings. MRS. WIENER *grabs it.*

> MRS. WIENER
> Hello? . . . Yes . . . oh . . . i-in Times Square? . . . Are you sure? . . . yes . . . thank you . . . (*Hangs up, returns to the table, weakly*) They found her tutu.

She breaks down sobbing.

EXT. WIENER HOME—NIGHT

DAWN *sneaks outside, running off with a plastic bag.*

EXT. STREET—NIGHT

A bus stops. DAWN *steps aboard and it takes off.*

EXT. NEW YORK CITY—PORN DISTRICT—NIGHT

TILT DOWN *from the bright lights of an X-rated movie house to* DAWN, *standing on the sidewalk. She is trying to hand out flyers with* MISSY's *picture to the men who pass by, but they are uninterested.*

> DAWN
> Excuse me. Have you seen my sister?

EXT. FORTUNE TELLER STOREFRONT—NIGHT

DAWN *walks up to a* FORTUNE TELLER *and shows her one of her Missy flyers.*

> DAWN
> Pardon me. Have you seen my sister? Her name is Missy Wiener.

> FORTUNE TELLER
> No.

EXT. CITY STREET—NIGHT

DAWN *plasters a wall with Missy flyers.*

EXT. BODEGA—NIGHT

DAWN *shows Missy flyers to* CARD PLAYERS *hanging out, but they don't recognize* MISSY.

EXT. CHINATOWN—NIGHT

DAWN *shows Missy flyers to* DOMINO PLAYERS, *but they haven't seen* MISSY *either.*

EXT. EAST VILLAGE—NIGHT

A HOMELESS MAN *accosts* DAWN *while she posts Missy flyers against a newsstand wall.*

DAWN

Have you seen my sister? Her name's Missy Wiener.

HOMELESS MAN

No!

EXT. MEATPACKING DISTRICT—NIGHT

DAWN, *getting tired, posts yet another Missy flyer, then trudges off.*

DISSOLVE TO:

EXT. STREET—NIGHT

DAWN *is sleeping by a subway gate.*

Suddenly she hears her sister calling. She looks up.

MISSY (o.s.)

Help! Dawn! Help me! Dawn! Dawn!

DAWN *sees* MISSY *being carried away by a* STRANGER.

DAWN

Missy?

MISSY

Help me! Help me! Dawn! Help . . . !

79

DAWN *jumps up and follows in hot pursuit.*

DAWN

Missy! Wait! Wait! Stop! Stop! Let go of my sister!

The STRANGER, *still holding* MISSY, *runs down a closed subway entrance.*

There is the sound of an oncoming train, then a crashing metal clang.

MISSY

Dawn!

MISSY *escapes up the subway stairs, embracing* DAWN *at the top.*

As if out of nowhere MRS. WIENER *suddenly appears and hugs* DAWN.

MRS. WIENER

Dawn! Dawn! Oh, Dawn! Oh, Dawn! You're the best daughter a mother could have!

DAWN'S POV:

MRS. WIENER

I love you so much!

MR. WIENER

(*In bed*) I love you, Dawn!

MARK

(*At his desk*) Me too. I love you.

BRANDON

(*At school*) Oh, Dawn. I love you.

STEVE

(*At the Wiener garage*) Dawn! I love you!

RALPHY

(*At the 7–11*) And you know I've always loved you.

STUDENTS

(*In the cafeteria*) Oh, Dawn! We love you!

EXT. STREET—MORNING

DAWN *suddenly wakes up. She looks around, sees a* HOMELESS MAN *scavenging in a dumpster.*

She rises, walks to a pay phone.

INT. WIENER HOME—MORNING

MARK *is at the breakfast table, eating cereal and reading his calculus book.* DETECTIVES, POLICEMEN, REPORTERS, CAMERA CREW PEOPLE *go about their business in the background.*

For the phone conversation, we cut back and forth between MARK *and* DAWN:

> MARK
>
> Yeah, I'll accept.

> DAWN
>
> Hi, Mark? It's Dawn.

> MARK
>
> Boy, are you in trouble. Where are you?

> DAWN
>
> New York.

> MARK
>
> What are you doing there?

> DAWN
>
> I-I ran away.

> MARK
>
> Are you serious?

> DAWN
>
> Yeah. I thought I might find Missy.

> MARK
>
> Way to go.

> DAWN
>
> Is Mom real upset?

MARK

Not really, actually. They found Missy this morning.

DAWN

Is she dead?

MARK

No, she's fine. It turns out Mr. Kasdan kidnapped her.

DAWN

Really?

MARK

Yeah. Mrs. Kasdan is probably gonna file for divorce now. Turns out he'd built this little underground room beneath the shuffleboard court and kept her there.

DAWN

Did he rape her?

MARK

Nah. I think he videotaped her doing some pirouettes, but that's it.

DAWN

Is she in the hospital?

MARK

No, she's here. And she's the same. Y'know, actually, I think she may have liked being there, 'cause she had her own TV and total control over the pusher. And she also got to have as much candy and McDonald's as she wanted.

DAWN

Can you get Mom?

MARK

Yeah, hold on. (*Calling*) Mom! It's Dawn!

MARK *gets up. He sees* MRS. WIENER *and* MISSY *sitting cuddled up on the sofa in the living room, posing for* REPORTERS *and* CAMERAMEN. *He realizes now might not be the best time.*

MARK
(*To* DAWN) Can you call back a little later? She's being inter-
viewed.

DAWN
Okay.

She hangs up, despondent.

MR. EDWARDS (v.o.)
. . . And now, students, I'd like you to give your attention . . .

INT. SCHOOL AUDITORIUM

MR. EDWARDS *stands at a lectern introducing* DAWN. *It is a full assembly.*

MR. EDWARDS
(*Continuing*) . . . to Dawn Wiener.

Polite applause.

DAWN *walks up to the lectern with a piece of paper and begins reading:*

DAWN
. . . I'm standing here today to express my and my family's
thanks for the support in helping . . . us get through this hor-
terrible ordeal. If it hadn't been for your help in providing the
police with the information leading to the conviction of Joseph
Kasdan, my sister might not be here today. Your emotional and
moral support has been invaluable.
    Missy has always been like . . . a sister to me . . . and a friend . . .

JED
(*Seated in the audience*) Wiener-dog!

TEACHER
Quiet!

DAWN
And now that she is safe and sound . . .

Now all the students join in the chant:

STUDENTS
Wiener-dog! Wiener-dog! Wiener-dog! . . .

DAWN

And now that she is safe and sound . . .

DAWN *tries to go on, but it is futile. The "Wiener-dog" chanting has become deafening, uncontrollable, frightening.*

Finally MR. EDWARDS *rises and shouts:*

MR. EDWARDS

QUIET!!!

Instant silence.

MR. EDWARDS

Go on, Dawn.

DAWN

(*Continuing where she left off, resisting the urge to break down and cry*). . . I can rest easy in the knowledge that . . . that Missy is fine. Thank you very much.

TV REPORTER (V.O.)

. . . were unavailable for comment.

INT. WIENER HOME—EVENING

The whole family is watching a "60 Minutes"-type news/interview show.

TV REPORTER (V.O.)

(*Continuing*) ". . . Friends and neighbors, however, shocked at his arrest, described Joseph Kasdan as a regular family man who would often dress up as Santa at Christmastime. And now we bring you an exclusive interview from our own Katie O'Neal . . .

During a shot of MR. KASDAN *being escorted away from his home by the police,* MARK *rises to go to the kitchen.*

MR. WIENER

While you're at it, can you get me another bag of popcorn?

MRS. WIENER

And a glass of Diet Coke!

MISSY

And Hawaiian Punch!

MARK *leaves.*

MISSY *and her parents sit raptly watching the TV interview:*

> TV REPORTER (o.s.)
> . . . Touch you at all in any way?

> MISSY ON TV (o.s.)
> I don't know.

> TV REPORTER (o.s.)
> Anyway, I bet you're happy to be home with Mommy . . .

> MISSY ON TV (o.s.)
> Yes.

DAWN *gets up and joins* MARK *in the kitchen. He is pouring juice.*

> TV REPORTER (o.s.)
> (*More remote now, less audible*) So tell me, Mrs. Wiener. How did you feel when you discovered . . .

> DAWN
> Mark, is eighth grade better than seventh?

> MARK
> Not really.

> DAWN
> What about ninth?

> MARK
> All of junior high school sucks. High school's better; it's closer to college. They'll call you names, but not as much to your face.

DAWN *steps away for a moment, notices the Hummingbirds Class Trip to Disney World flyer thumbtacked to the bulletin board.*

> DAWN
> I don't want to go to Disney World.

> MARK
> Don't be stupid. If nothing else, it'll look good on your college resume.

He returns to the TV room.

85

HUMMINGBIRDS (V.O.)
(*Singing*) Look in the sky at the tiny birds that fly . . .

EXT. HIGHWAY—DAY

A bus speeds by.

HUMMINGBIRDS (V.O.)
(*Continuing*) . . . With wings that move faster than the eye can
see . . .

INT. BUS—DAY

DAWN *and the rest of the Hummingbirds are singing "The Humming-bird Anthem." As the* CAMERA DOLLIES *down the bus aisle to find* DAWN, *we see that for her the effort to sing cheerfully is a little greater than for her classmates. When the* CAMERA *finishes* ZOOMING *in to her, it is her voice alone that we hear.*

HUMMINGBIRDS
(*Continuing*) Hummingbirds!
Hooray! Hurrah! Sis-boom-bah!
Now put on a smile, kids
Wipe off that frown
We're hummable hummingbirds
Happy and sunny birds humming all day long
Come and join us in our song!
Hum!
Hummable hummingbirds humming along we are
Hum!
Hummable hummingbirds
We go up up up into the sky
We're the Hummingbirds of Benjamin Franklin Junior High
Hum!

CUT TO BLACK

1984   *Feelings* (New York University short)
1984   *Babysitter* (NYU short)
1985   *Schatt's Last Shot* (NYU short)
1986   *How I Became a Leading Artistic Figure in New York City's East Village Cultural Landscape* ("Saturday Night Live" short)
1989   *Fear, Anxiety, and Depression* (Goldwyn)
1996   *Welcome to the Dollhouse* (Sony Pictures Classics)